DEWDROPS

Daily Quote from the Holy Mother

Sri Ramakrishna Math
Mylapore, Chennai - 4

Published by Adhyaksha, Sri Ramakrishna Math, Mylapore, Chennai - 4

First Edition, December 2014; Second Print, September 2016
2M3C

ISBN: 978-81-7883-591-4

Total number of copies printed till now: 2,300

Printed in India at Sri Ramakrishna Math Printing Press Mylapore, Chennai - 4

Preface

Holy Mother Sri Sarada Devi stands as a source of peace and comfort in this ephemeral world with innumerable troubles and tensions. Born on 21 December 1853 in a small village called Jayarambati in West Bengal, the Holy Mother is being celebrated as an ideal woman and ideal mother.

Married to Sri Ramakrishna at the age of five, she imbibed the great ideals her husband stood for. As husband and wife, they led a pure life without any physical dimension to their relationship. In fact, Sri Ramakrishna worshipped her as the Divine Mother Herself.

After the mahasamadhi of Sri Ramakrishna, the Holy Mother continued the work initiated by him. She had to bear all the trials and tribulations attendant with poverty and widowhood. But she took it all as part of her spiritual strivings and ministrations.

Her prayer to Sri Ramakrishna on seeing his monastic disciples wander about without any permanent shelter bore fruit in the form of establishing the Ramakrishna Math and Mission. She was a loving mother, caring guide and venerable guru for innumerable disciples, both monastic and lay. She attained mahasamadhi on 20 July 1920 after demonstrating in her life the ideal of motherhood.

The conversations the Holy Mother had had with her disciples and devotees have been compiled in the book *The Gospel of Holy Mother* published by our Math.

A booklet *Dinam Or Anbumozhi* in Tamil containing the datewise compilation of selected teachings of the Holy Mother culled from her *Gospel* was published by our Math in 2011. Sri Maniam Selvan, Smt. Pushpa Chitrak, Sri Natarajan and Sri Ravi had designed the cover page, sketches and layout.

To benefit a larger section of the devotees, we are bringing out an English version of that booklet with some modifications, titling it as ***Dewdrops***.

We are grateful to Smt. Latha Balasubramaniam for helping us in the compilation of these quotations. We pray to the Holy Mother to bless her and all others who have contributed to the preparation of this booklet.

May we begin our day with a dewdrop of the Holy Mother!

Sri Ramakrishna Math
Mylapore, Chennai - 4

Holy Mother Sri Sarada Devi Jayanti
13 December 2014

Mother has been born to revive that wonderful Shakti in India; and making her the nucleus, once more will Gargis and Maitreyis be born into the world... Without the grace of Shakti nothing is to be accomplished.

Swami Vivekananda

I bless you on this holy day that you may attain to liberation in this life. Birth and death are extremely painful. May you not suffer from them any more!

Neither mantra nor scripture is of any avail; bhakti or devotion alone accomplishes everything. Sri Ramakrishna is everything—both Guru and Ishta. He is all in all.

God resides in the human body, but man does not know it. Therefore he searches everywhere for bliss, not knowing that it is already in him. God alone is real. All else is false.

The Master is the Supreme God and the Supreme Goddess. He is the essence of all mantras, the embodiment of all deities, and dwells in all creatures. One can worship all the gods and goddesses in and through him.

Pray to God with tears in your eyes whenever you want illumination or find yourself faced with any doubt or difficulty. The Lord will remove all your impurities, assuage your mental anguish, and give you enlightenment.

It is in the mind alone that one feels pure or impure. A man first makes his own mind guilty and then sees another's fault. Can you injure anybody by enumerating his faults? You only injure yourself.

In earlier days I also had an eye for people's faults. Thereafter I wept and wept before the Master, praying, 'O Master! I do not wish to see anyone's faults' and finally got rid of that habit.

Do not fear, my child. Always remember that the Master is behind you. I am also with you. As long as you remember me, your mother, why should you be frightened?

My child, this mind is just like a wild elephant. It races with the wind. Therefore one should discriminate all the time. One should work hard for the realization of God.

I don't know anything. I repeat only what I have heard from the Master. Read the Gospel [of Sri Ramakrishna] and you will know all you need.

One should always be active. One should never be without work. For when one is idle, all sorts of bad thoughts crop up in one's mind.

If you love any human being you will have to suffer for it. He is blessed, indeed, who can love God alone. There is no suffering in loving God.

I am the mother of the wicked, as I am the mother of the virtuous. Never fear. Whenever you are in distress, just say to yourself, 'I have a mother.'

As you pray and meditate...you will realize that He who is in me, is in you too and in the humblest of men—only then humility will be born in your mind.

People complain about their griefs and sorrows and how they pray to God but find no relief from pain. But grief itself is a gift from God. It is symbol of His compassion.

You should certainly repeat the mantra also. However, calling upon God with one's mind steadfast is equivalent to a million repetitions of the mantra.

What is the good in doing japa for a whole day if there is no concentration of mind? Collectedness of one's mind is essential, and then only His grace descends.

True it is that there is no hard and fast rule about the time of japa, yet morning and evening are the favourable periods. Whatever the time be, you must do japa every day. It is not good to forgo it any day.

One should meditate on one's Chosen Deity as one goes on making japa. In meditation, the face of the Chosen Deity of course comes first, but one should meditate on the whole figure, starting from the feet upward.

Read a small portion of the Gita daily and also the Gospel of the Master and Portrait [of Sri Ramakrishna]. Many other books about the Master have also been published. Read them.

As a result of obsession the mind never feels pure. An impure mind does not easily become pure. The more you emphasize your obsession, the more obsessed you become. It is true of all things.

In time the mind itself becomes the Guru. To pray to God and meditate on Him for two minutes with full concentration is better than doing so for long hours without it.

Where else is God except very close to His devotees? If worldly people even visit the place used by holy men, the very atmosphere of the place can remove the dross of their mind.

One must bear with everything, because everything is determined by actions (Karmas). Again, our present actions can counteract the effect of past actions.

Most obstacles in worship are not external; they are internal. They will gradually fall off one after another by taking the Master's name and by meditation.

Each has to get the results of the actions he earned for this life. A pin at least must prick where a wound from a sword was due.

In these miserable times one may find God only through steadfast truth. The Master used to say, 'He who clings to truth, lies in the lap of God.'

In one word, one should desire of God desirelessness. For desire alone is at the root of all suffering. It is the cause of repeated births and deaths. It is the obstacle in the way of liberation.

Does it matter in the least to God whether you believe or not? Even the sage Shuka Deva was to Him like a big ant at the most. Infinite is He. How much can you understand of Him?

Does one get faith by mere studying books? Too much reading creates confusion. The Master used to say that one should learn from the scriptures that God alone is real and the world illusory.

What an illusion Mahamaya has conjured up! Here is this infinite world, and what one claims as one's possession will be left behind at death. Still men cannot understand this simple truth.

If you want the grace of Sri Ramakrishna, first propitiate the Mother. The Mother is the supreme Primordial Power Herself (Parama Prakriti). She holds the key of the knowledge of Brahman in her hand.

Swami Brahmananda

Is it possible always [to remember Mother's real nature]? If it were so, can all this work go on? Yet amidst all this work whenever the desire arises, inspiration comes in a flash upon a little thought and the whole of the play of Mahamaya comes to be understood.

The Master used to say, 'The way is extremely difficult, like the sharp edge of a razor.' But he has kept you in his arms. He is looking after you.

Everything, no doubt, happens by God's will, yet man must work because God expresses His will through man's action. Do not relax your spiritual practices.

What is there in this world? Tell me what is good in this life?
That was why in the end the Master took only bitter things.
I would try to give him sandesh and he would say,
'What is there in sandesh? It is just the same as clay.'

Do you notice this human body? Today it is and tomorrow it is not. And the world is full of misery and pain. Why should one be eager to have another birth?
The body is never free from its attendant troubles.

Don't be afraid. I tell you that in this Kali Yuga mental sin is no sin. Free your mind from all worries on this account. You need not be afraid.

Everything is due to desire. What bondage is there for a man who has no desire? You see, I live with all these things, but I do not feel any attachment; no, not in the least.

They (the monks) are like white cloth, whereas the worldly people are like black cloth on which even ink-spots do not show, but a single spot on the white material catches the eye. To be in the body is a source of evil.

Free yourself from all anxiety by entrusting your future to me. And remember this always that there is one behind you who will come to you at the right moment and lead you to the everlasting domain.

I want people here who are careful in work. There are those who perform great deeds on the spur of the moment. But a man can be really known from the interest he shows in the details of each duty.

Service, in the real sense of the word, is not a joke. One should be extremely careful about making His service perfectly flawless. But the truth is, God knows our foolishness and therefore He forgives us.

Everyone must experience the consequence of his past actions. Nevertheless, the remembrance of God's name helps one this much—instead of losing a leg, one may suffer merely from a thorn entering one's foot.

Don't let your mind be disturbed over these trivial details. That will make you forget the Master. Whatever people may say, remember the Master and do what you consider to be right.

Is life in the world separate from God? He is everywhere. Besides, you are a woman; where will you go, dear? Be content with wherever and in whatever situation He places you. The goal is to call upon Him and to attain to Him. If you call upon Him, He will lead you by the hand. You will have no fear if you can depend on Him.

How much intelligence does a man possess? He is likely to ask for something other than what he really needs. He may even end up creating a monkey in place of Siva. It is wise to take refuge in Him. He will always give you whatever is necessary. However, one should pray for devotion and desirelessness; for such a prayer does no harm.

Many may take the name of God after their minds have been hardened by the contaminating influence of the world. But he is blessed indeed who can devote himself to God from his very childhood.

One can postpone a holy duty out of considerations of time, but look; Death (Kala) takes no notice of time. Since Death has no fixed hours, one should perform holy duties as soon as an opportunity comes.

What else is spiritual life besides praying to the Master, repeating his name and contemplating him? And the Master? What is there, after all, about him? He is our own eternally.

Nobody does any japa regularly. Some don't do it even once. Yet as I have shouldered the burden, should I not look after them? That's why I do japa and pray to the Master.

The household is the Lord's, and so in whatever work He has placed you, you should, depending entirely upon Him, do your best to perform it well.

Besides Brahman there is nothing else in this world. Everything that appears before us is the manifestation of Brahman. It is its power, which is present in all gods and goddesses.

To call upon Him at the conjunction of day and night is the most auspicious. Night disappears and day arrives, or day disappears and night arrives—this is the conjunction of day and night. The mind remains pure at these times.

You see, only those who belong to a high spiritual category can become monks and liberate themselves from all kinds of fetters. Some, again, are born just to enjoy the world. I say, it is good to finish in entirety enjoyments and sufferings.

Those who have come here remembering the Master will certainly have the vision of their Chosen Ideal. Even if one does not have it during his lifetime, he will assuredly have it at least just before his death.

You see, my dear, many people seek God only after disappointment in other spheres. But he, who from childhood, can place at the Master's feet a heart as pure as a flower, is blessed indeed!

Free yourself from all anxiety by entrusting your future to me. And remember this always, that there is one behind you who will come to you at the right moment and lead you to the everlasting domain.

Give up this dry discussion, this hodgepodge of philosophy. Who has been able to know God by reasoning? Even sages like Shuka and Vyasa are at best like big ants trying to carry away a few grains of sugar from a large heap.

One must live carefully. Every action produces its results. It is not good to use harsh words towards others or be responsible for their suffering.

If you don't call upon God — indeed many people never even remember Him — what does it matter to Him?
It is your own misfortune.

Mother assumed this human body in order to awaken the entire womanhood of the world. Don't you see, after her advent, what amazing awakening has set forth among the womankind of the world?

Swami Shivananda

Can everybody recognize an Incarnation? One or two persons only can recognize him. How much suffering do they undergo for the liberation of human beings! Even when the Master used to vomit blood, he never stopped speaking. He was all the while worried about the well-being of people.

Man knows in his own mind how far he has advanced and how much knowledge and consciousness of God he has attained. He knows in his innermost soul how much of God he has realized.

I cannot see others' faults. I am simply not made that way. There are enough people always ready to criticize others. Surely the world will not come to an end if I refrain from doing so.

In this Kali Yuga one attains to God if one simply sticks to truth. He who speaks nothing but truth is resting on the lap of God!

Don't fear, my child. The Master will look after you. He will watch over you here and hereafter. He will protect you always.

Where is that competent student who can understand spiritual instruction? First of all, one should be fit; otherwise, the instructions prove futile.

Why do you fear? The Master himself will do everything for those who have received his blessings or have somehow come in contact with him.

Spiritual practices are meant to keep the mind steady at the feet of God, to keep it immersed in His thought. Repeat His Name.

From time immemorial so many people have practised image-worship and thereby got liberation. Do you mean to say that is nothing?

Can you call him a man who is devoid of compassion? He is a veritable beast. Sometimes I forget myself in compassion. Then I do not remember who I am.

Even the injunctions of destiny are cancelled if one takes refuge in God. Destiny strikes off with her own hand what she has written about such a person.

Whenever you go from one place to another, observe the things around you, and also keep yourself well-informed about what happens in the place where you live. But keep your lips shut.

Whenever you go on some work, make it a point to return as soon as it is finished. In this life you will find that in digging for earthworms we often go deeper and bring out snakes.

No one will suffer for all time. No one will spend all his days on this earth in suffering. Every action brings its own result and one gets one's opportunities accordingly.

The creation itself is full of misery and happiness. Could anyone appreciate happiness if misery did not exist? Besides, how is it possible for all persons to be happy?

Illness is not within man's control. And if you are really tied down with work, then simply remember God and make salutation to Him.

God realization can be had at any time by the grace of God, but there is a difference between it and what comes in the fullness of time.

Don't worry! Restlessness is the nature of the mind, as it is of the eyes and ears. Practise regularly. The Name of God is more powerful than the senses. Always think of the Master, who is looking after you. Don't be troubled about your lapses.

Sit for meditation in the morning and the evening. Keep your head cool and practise meditation and prayer. It is very difficult to do so. It is rather easy to dig the earth with a spade... You will achieve nothing without His grace.

As long as a man has desires, there is no end to his transmigration. It is the desires alone that make him take one body after another.

Please do not worry so much, my child. Let the will of God be done. You have been following the right path. The Lord will never put you to any difficulty.

One suffers as a result of one's own actions. So, instead of blaming others for such sufferings, one should pray to the Lord and depending entirely on His grace, try to bear them patiently and with forbearance under all circumstances.

How many are there who truly want to realize God? Where is that earnestness? They no doubt profess great devotion and longing, but they feel satisfied when they get even a tiny bit of enjoyment. They say, 'Ah, how kind is God!'

One must be patient like the earth. What iniquities are being perpetrated on her! Yet she quietly endures them all. Man too should be like that.

Human being—today he is, tomorrow he is not. No one will accompany a person after his death. Only his actions—good and bad—follow him, even after death.

While performing japa, take the Name of God with utmost love, sincerity, and self-surrender. Before commencing your meditation daily, first think of your utter helplessness in this world and then slowly begin the practice of sadhana as directed by your Guru.

Do not fear, my child. Always remember that the Master is behind you. I am also with you. As long as you remember me, your mother, why should you be frightened?

The Master said to me, 'In the end I shall certainly liberate those who come to you.'

One shouldn't lose oneself so much in uttering. If one sees the worst of everything, one feels pain. 'X' has got into such a habit of speaking out the truth that she no longer cares about what others will think. I, on the other hand, still care. One should never indulge in unpleasant truths.

Through spiritual disciplines like japa the ties of past Karma are cut asunder. But realization of God cannot be achieved without ecstatic love (Prema Bhakti) for Him. Do you know the significance of japa and other spiritual practices? By these, the dominance of the sense organs is subdued.

Will a man who has strong desires for worldly pleasures listen to me if I ask him to renounce them? But if a fortunate soul has realized the world to be the sport of Maya and God alone to be real, shall I not help him a little? Is there any end to the suffering in the world?

You will gain everything if you but take refuge in the Master. Renunciation alone was his splendour. We utter his name and eat and enjoy things because he renounced all. People think that his devotees also must be very great, as he was a man of such complete renunciation.

We could get some inkling at least of the greatness of the Master (Sri Ramakrishna), but of this lady we cannot understand anything. She has drawn the veil of Maya so thick around Her that no one can see through it and have a glimpses of Her greatness.

Swami Saradananda

Do your duty. Don't pay attention to whether the blemishes of the mind are persisting or not. The branch of a cocoanut tree drops off by itself at the proper time, but one has to exert much to tear off the branch before the proper time arrives. Likewise, everything will come about at the proper time.

One must live very carefully. Every action produces its results. It is not good to harass others or use harsh words towards others.

If you do a good action, that will counteract your past evil action. Past sins can be counteracted by meditation, japa and spiritual thought.

Is the value of a thing to be gauged by its price? It is the love and devotion with which a thing is offered that really counts.

Whose work are you doing? It is His work only. In time to come, your mind itself will turn into your Guru and advise you.

Our Master was a man of direct perception. He saw everything; he knew everything. His words are the words of the Veda. What will you do if you do not believe in his words?

We must pray for Nirvasana, freedom from desire. Desire is at the root of all sorrows, the cause of repeated births and deaths, and the main obstacle on the path of liberation.

There is great complexity in this creation. The Master does one thing through one man and another thing through another person. Oh, it is so inscrutable!

One should practise japa with some devotion, but this is not done. They will not do anything, they will only complain, saying, 'Why do I not succeed?'

Is it possible, my child, to get of vanity — vanity of beauty, vanity of virtue, vanity of knowledge and vanity of a holy life?

Each has to get the results of the actions he earned for this life. A pin at least must prick where a wound from a sword was due.

What else shall you do if you do not believe in the words of high-souled men? Is there any other way except the one trodden by sages and seers and other holy men?

Such is life, here today, gone tomorrow! Nothing goes with one, except one's merit and demerit; good and evil deeds follow one even after death.

What else does a man obtain by the realization of God? Does he grow two horns? No, his mind becomes pure, and through such a pure mind one attains knowledge and spiritual awakening.

[To a woman disciple] Never be intimate with any man, not even your own father or brother. What to speak of others then! Let me again repeat: don't be intimate with any man, even if God comes to you in that form.

I say to the Master, 'O Lord! In this world and in the next, you alone have to save them.' Where is the yearning? They speak so much of their devotion and earnestness on the one hand, and on the other they are so pleased with any little enjoyment they come to have.

Keep a picture of the Master before you, and know for certain that he is always with you. Open your grief-stricken heart to him. Shed tears and sincerely pray, 'O Lord, draw me towards you, give me peace of mind.' By doing so constantly you will gradually attain peace of mind.

It is not that you will not face difficulties. They will arise. But they will not remain. You will see that they pass away like water under one's feet.

The Master used to say, 'At the time of death I shall have to stand by those who pray to me.' These are words from his own mouth.

A person may have not relatives anywhere, but Mahamaya may make him keep a cat and thus make him worldly. This is how She plays!

Along with work, if you do not meditate morning and evening, how can you understand whether you are working on the right lines?

The Master is the basis of all that we are. He is the ideal. You will never take a false step if you hold onto him under all circumstances.

Can anyone altogether destroy lust? A little of it remains as long as one has the body. But it can be subdued, as a snake can be subdued by charmed dust.

What do you mean? You won't do japa of your mantra? What a suggestion! If you don't do the japa, you lose; that affects me not in the least!

Repeat the Name of God; whether your mind is concentrated or not it will be good for you if you can repeat the name of God for a fixed number of times every day.

To cast the image means to meditate and contemplate on the Master, to think of the various incidents of his life. By meditating on him, one gets all the spiritual moods.

Women should not get angry so easily. They must practise forbearance. In infancy and childhood their parents are their only protection and in youth their husbands.

Why should not one have concentration and meditation if the mind is pure? Why should not one have God vision? When one sits down for japa, God's Name will continue rising up from the mind naturally and not with effort.

If you want peace of mind then give up fault-finding. If you would search for fault at all, find out your own faults and shortcomings. Learn to accept everyone as your own. No one is alien to you, the whole world is yours.

Such is the fascination of money that if you involve yourself too much in it, you will feel attracted to it. You may think that you are above money and that you will never feel any attraction for it, as you have renounced it. You may further think that at any moment you may leave it behind. No, my child, never harbor this thought in your mind.

May

The exalted empress has of her own accord appeared as the indigent woman. She sweeps floors, scours vessels, husks paddy and even removes the leaving of devotees after food... in order to teach the householders their duties.

Swami Premananda

Why can't one meditate if one has a pure mind? Why should one not be able to see God? When a pure soul performs japa, he feels as if the holy Name bubbles up spontaneously from within himself. He does not make an effort to repeat the Name.

God is like a child, you know. He denies some who seek and of Himself gives to some who do not. Perhaps such people had highly evolved souls from their previous lives. That is why they receive His grace.

It is essential that one should work. It is through work alone that one may break asunder the bonds of Karma; only then is one free from desires. One shouldn't be without work even for a single moment.

You might have done good to a man a thousand times and harm only once; he will turn away from you for that one offence. People see only the faults. One should in fact note the merits.

There are people who perform wonderful deeds under momentary excitement. But a man's true worth can be known only by observing the attention he bestows on his daily inconsequential actions.

Should one speak such words as would hurt the feelings of another? Even if it is truth, it should not be told in an unpleasant manner. Finally, you will end up with that kind of nature. If one's sensitivity is lost, then nothing would control one's speech.

Flowers are best used in the service of the Lord. Otherwise it is better that they fade away on the trees. I feel very bad when I see foppish gentlemen make sometimes a bouquet of flowers or sometimes casually put a flower to their nose and admire, 'Ah! What fine scent!'

However great a soul may be, when he assumes a mortal body, he must bear all bodily sorrows. The only difference is that ordinary people depart in tears, but a great soul goes laughing as though death were a game.

One should not trifle with a thing though it may be very insignificant. If you respect a thing, the thing also respects you. Even a broomstick should be treated with respect. One should perform even an insignificant work with respect.

As long as man has desires, there is no end to his transmigration. It is desires that make him take one body after another. There will be rebirth for a man if he has even the desire to eat a piece of candy.

We should give everyone his due. What is not edible for a man, give to a cow; what is not edible for a cow, give to a dog; what is not edible for a dog, throw into a lake for fishes to eat. But never waste.

Spiritual discipline means holding the mind steadfast at His holy feet all the time and immersing the mind in thoughts of Him. Repeat His Name.

Far better is it to work than to let the mind loose to indulge in riotous thinking. If the mind is allowed a little laxity, it will create such a turmoil.

The mind will be steadied if one repeats the Name of God fifteen or twenty thousand times a day. It is truly so. Let them practise it first, if they fail, let them complain.

My child, austerities or worship, practise all these things right now. Will these things be possible later on? Whatever you want to achieve, achieve now; this is the right time.

Along with work, if you do not meditate morning and evening, how can you understand whether you are working on the right lines?

Know that service to your mother is your highest duty. But it is a different matter if she stands in the way of your spiritual progress.

Whenever you feel your mind stirred by undesirable thoughts and yet you desire knowledge, pray to Him earnestly. He will purify your mind and solve your doubts.

With so much earnestness they take initiation. But why then are they not practising anything? Is it so difficult to do so? With a little practice one gets such joy!

Don't puzzle the mind with too many inquiries. One finds it difficult to put one single thing into practice, but dares invite distraction by filling the mind with too many things.

The mantra purifies the body. Man becomes pure by repeating the mantra of God. It is said, 'The human teacher utters the mantra into the ear; but God breathes the spirit into the soul.'

He [the Master] used to say, 'One who remembers me never suffers from want of food or from other physical privations.' ...

By remembering him one gets rid of all sufferings.

If one calls upon Him repeatedly, He becomes compassionate; and so a devoted attachment comes into being. This love for love's sake should be hidden from all eyes.

If a person is steady in meditation, he will clearly see the Lord in his heart and hear His voice. The moment an idea flashes in his mind, it will at once be fulfilled and he will be bathed in peace.

To err is human. One must not take that into account. It is harmful for oneself. One gets into the habit of finding fault... Do not look for faults in others, or your own eyes will become faulty.

Have intense devotion to God. One must work hard. How can one achieve anything without effort? You must devote some time for prayer even in the midst of the busiest hour of the day.

Only through work can one remove the bondage of work. Total detachment comes later. One should not be without work even for a moment. Work helps one to fend off idle thoughts.

If you practise spiritual discipline for some time in a solitary place, you will find that your mind has become strong, and then you can live in any place or society without being in the least affected by it.

In the fullness of spiritual realization, a person finds that the God who resides in his heart resides in the hearts of all—the oppressed, the persecuted, the lowly, and the untouchable.
This realization makes one truly humble.

My child, whatever one is, if he comes in the garb of a sannyasin, you do sadhu seva (service to holy people) by offering him something or serving him in some way.

People find opportunities according to their fate and Karma... The fact is, if one's time to go beyond the world is ripe, one will break all bonds and come; nobody will check him.

June

Blessed is the Mother's grace! How great is her fortitude! Not the slightest trace of annoyance about her. Day and night, incessantly people are coming, and she is doing good to them unstintedly.

Swami Turiyananda

It is quite natural that man forgets God. Therefore whenever the need arises, God Himself incarnates on earth and shows the path by Himself practising sadhana. This time (taking the avatara of Sri Ramakrishna) he has also shown the example of renunciation.

Child, this is the law of nature [regarding weakness of the mind]. Have you not noticed the full moon and the new moon? Likewise the mind is sometimes dominated by good, and sometimes by bad tendencies.

Love alone is the essential thing. Our organization is growing only through love... They are my children and have taken shelter with Sri Ramakrishna. Wherever they go, the Master will look after them.

You will play the true role of a son only if you can help your mother acquire the means for her higher evolution in the hereafter.

No doubt you must do your duties. This keeps your mind in good condition. But it is also necessary to practise japa, meditation, and prayer.

Do japa and meditation. The practice of meditation will lead your mind to such one-pointedness that you won't like to give up meditation.

Look, do not try to start a sensation by shouting vande mataram. Rather you should make looms and weave cloth. I wish to spin thread if I can get a spinning wheel. Do constructive work.

On moonlit nights I would look at the moon and pray, 'May my mind be pure as the rays of the moon!' or 'O Lord, there are stains even on the moon, but let my mind be absolutely stainless.'

When I was at Vrindavan, I used to visit Vankubihari (Krishna in a bent pose) and prayed to him, 'Your form is bent, but Your mind is straight—kindly straighten the windings of my mind.'

Don't give up your practice of japa, even if your mind doesn't become steady. Do your spiritual practice ardently. Repeating His name will make your mind steadfast like the flame of a lamp protected from wind. Wind makes a flame unsteady. Similarly, desires prevent the mind from becoming concentrated.

Practise meditation regularly, for your mind is still unripe. After prolonged practice of meditation your mind will become steady. And you should constantly discriminate between the real and the unreal. Know the worldly objects to which the mind is drawn to be unreal and surrender your mind to God.

In course of time one does not feel even the existence of God. After attaining wisdom (Jnana) one sees that gods and deities are all maya. Everything comes into existence in time and also disappears in time.

To call upon Him at the conjunction of day and night is the most auspicious. Night disappears and day arrives, or day disappears and night arrives—this is the conjunction of day and night. The mind remains pure at these times.

Whenever any evil thought haunts you, tell your mind: 'Being her child, can I stoop so low as to indulge in any such activity?' You will find that you gain strength and peace of mind.

Regarding family people who wanted to renounce worldly life, Mother said, 'If you really want to give up, first make suitable arrangements for the subsistence of your dependents.'

God has the nature of a child. Some beg but He does not give them, while others do not want but He asks them to accept. Perhaps the latter had many meritorious acts to their credit in their past births. Therefore God's grace descends on them.

Whatever the Master has said about anyone will come to pass, come what may. His words cannot be falsified. Whether or not the person has desires in his present state, the Master had foreseen that in the end, all the desires will leave such a person.

We are here for this purpose only. If we do not accept others' sins and sorrows and digest them, who else will? Who else will bear the responsibility for sinners and sufferers?

Everybody reaps the fruit of his actions according to his past impressions and deeds. No doubt the sun is one, but its shining varies according to the place and the objects it illumines.

Observing the rules and injunctions prescribed by the Master, if one calls upon one's Chosen Ideal with steadfastness, one achieves everything.

Pray to the Master. I am with you. Know that you have already achieved liberation in this very birth. Why do you fear? In time he will do everything for you.

If the disciple commits a sin, that affects the Guru too. On the other hand, the Guru is benefited if the disciple is good.

Nobody should be saluted during his illness. Yes, my child, pranam made in such circumstances fixes the disease in the person.

It does not become a woman to argue like that. Even the wise could hardly realize the nature of Brahman by argument. Is Brahman an object of discussion?

Pray to God with all your might. One has to work. Can anything be achieved without work? Even in the midst of household duties one must make time for prayer.

The house may have all kinds of food-stuff for cooking, but one must cook them and take his meal. He who cooks earlier gets his meal earlier too. Some eat in the morning, some in the evening, and there are yet others who starve because they are lazy and reluctant to cook.

These are no real desires [insignificant desires]. They are nothing. They are mere fancies that appear and disappear in your mind. The more they come and go, the better for you. ...So long as the ego exists, desires also undoubtedly remain. But those desires will not injure you.

Will they abstain because of my prohibition if their desire for enjoyment is strong? And to those who have understood by virtue of great merit that all this is Maya's play, and believe that God alone is the reality, should I not offer a little help and encouragement? Is there any end to the miseries of the world?

Prayers please the Mother Peaceful. She is Vidya-maya. By taking refuge in her one gets rid of the darkness of Avidya-maya. When the Mother is propitiated, Sri Ramakrishna, being pleased, showers his grace on the devotee.

Swami Abhedananda

Our Master alone is Maheshvara (Supreme God) and Maheshvari (Supreme Goddess) as well. He alone is the embodiment of all Deities. He alone is the embodiment of all mystic syllables. One can worship through him all Gods and Goddesses. You can address him as Maheshvara as well as Maheshvari.

Our Master did not know much of reading and writing. The real thing is devotion to God... The Master was born on earth this time to liberate all, the rich and the poor, the learned and the illiterate.

Do not make any distinction between Sri Ramakrishna and me. Meditate on and pray to the particular aspect of the Divinity revealed to you. Worship ends with absorption in meditation.

The world is a great mire. If one gets into it, he finds it difficult to get free. Have deep faith in Him. Know the Master to be your refuge, just as parents are to children in this world.

Holy men are born on earth to show people the way to God. They teach differently. There are many paths leading to the same goal. Therefore the teachings of all the saints are true.

However much of japa you do, however much of work you perform all is for nothing. If Mahamaya does not open the way, is anything possible for anyone? O bound soul! Surrender, surrender, surrender. Then alone will She take compassion on you and leave your path open.

How much intelligence does a man possess? He is likely to ask for something other than what he really needs. He may even end up creating a monkey in place of Siva.

It is wise to take refuge in Him. He will always give you whatever is necessary.

Man is bound to make mistakes. One should not notice them. If one does not follow this rule, it harms oneself alone. By constantly observing the faults of others, in the end one will become a mere fault-finder.

Many think of God only after receiving blows from the world. But blessed indeed is he who can offer his mind, like a fresh flower, at the feet of the Lord from his very childhood.
One should practise renunciation in youth.

From desire comes this body into being. When there is no desire at all, the body falls away. With complete cessation of desires there comes the final end.

Those who are born to God have already fulfilled all their desires. So long as a man has any desire, he is incapable of such (motiveless) devotion.

If you want peace immediately, practise the spiritual discipline prescribed. Otherwise you will achieve it only after the fall of the body.

Can one get everything merely by meditating for a few days? Nothing will be of any avail unless Mahamaya clears the way.

Lay the burden of your mind before Sri Ramakrishna. Tell him your sorrows with your tears. You will find that he will fill up your arms with the desired object.

A single utterance of God's name is as effective as a million repetitions of it, if only you do it with a steady, concentrated mind.

The Master used to say that truthfulness alone is the austerity of the present age. One attains to God by holding to the truth.

God alone is eternally true. If one can call on Him, it is good. Taking a body one has to suffer from its accompanying troubles!

Those who have come here, those who are my children, have already achieved liberation. Even God can do no harm to my children.

What else will you do? Do what you are doing now. Remember that the Master is behind everyone of you. I too am behind you.

Always try to do God's work and at the same time try to practise japa and meditation. If you do such work, your mind will not be obsessed with evil thoughts. If you sit alone idly, all sorts of thoughts may come and disturb you mind.

Don't relax practise, simply because you do not get His vision. Does an angler catch a big carp everyday, the moment he sits with the rod? He has to wait and wait, and many a time he is disappointed.

The Master has predetermined what he is going to accomplish. If anyone surrenders himself totally at his feet, then the Master will see that everything is set right.

Repetition of His name will lead to the goal. Even when your mind does not become concentrated you can repeat the Holy Name thousands of times.

If one initiates somebody, one has to take his sins upon oneself. I feel that since the body must perish one day, let it be for the sake of these people.

Karma is exhausted gradually. When one realizes God, He endows one with spiritual illumination within. One becomes aware of it oneself.

Desire maybe compared to a minute seed. It is like a big banyan tree growing out of a seed, which is no bigger than a dot.

Numerous ordinary people are born, and die. The greatest souls accompany an incarnation of God in order to do His work.

Everything is real. Nothing is untrue. The Master is all—he is Prakriti, he is Purusha. Through him you will achieve everything.

Whatever may happen to you now, the Master will have to appear at the last moment of your life to receive you. He himself said this.

Many are known to do great works under the stress of some strong emotion. But a man's true nature is known from the manner in which he does his insignificant daily task.

We were all surprised to see the spirit of Sri Ramakrishna unified with her. It was unique. We realised that the Master and the Mother were one in essence, though appearing in separate forms.

Swami Yogananda

*Is life in the world separate from God? He is everywhere... Be content with wherever and in whatever situation He places you. The goal is to call upon Him and to attain to Him.
If you call upon Him, He will lead you by the hand.
You will have no fear if you can depend on Him.*

Always discriminate. Try to realize that the outside object which is attracting your mind is impermanent, and turn your attention to God

Practise meditation, and by and by your mind will be so calm and fixed that you will find it hard to keep away from meditation.

The Master will grant only those desires which you really need and which will bring you good. Continue to practise what you are doing now. Why fear? We are with you.

It is a great fortune to be the mother of a monk. But people cannot give up attachment to even a brass pot; how could they then think of renouncing the world?

He (Sri Ramakrishna) is the Godhead and one's Chosen Deity; he is all the gods and all their sacred word-symbols; in him one worships all the gods and goddesses. It does not matter how you address him.

Never fear, He is ever looking after you. Do His work and practise sadhana. A little work daily drives away idle thoughts from the mind. A solitary and inactive life is liable to be troubled with idle thinking.

What does a man become by realizing God? Does he get two horns? No. What happens is, he develops discrimination between the real and the unreal, gets spiritual illumination.

My child, you have been extremely fortunate in getting this human birth. Have intense devotion to God. One must work hard. How can one achieve anything without effort?

Open your grief-stricken heart to the Lord. Weep and sincerely pray, 'O Lord, draw me towards You; give me peace of mind.' By doing so constantly you will gradually attain peace of mind.

You see, my son, it is not a fact that you will never face dangers. Difficulties always come but they do not last forever. You will see that they pass away like water under a bridge.

One who makes a habit of prayer will easily overcome all difficulties and remain calm and unruffled in the midst of the trials of life.

These earthly ties are transitory. Today they seem to be the be-all and end-all of life, and tomorrow they vanish.
Your real tie is with God.

It is a complex always to be suspecting impurities. The more you emphasize your obsession, the more obsessed you become. It is true of all things.

Many turn towards God as a result of much suffering in life. But one whose mind is offered like a flower to the Lord right from childhood is indeed blessed.

The happiness of the world is transitory. The less you become attached to the world, the more you enjoy peace of mind.

Always do your duty to others, but love you must give to God alone. Worldly love always brings in its wake untold misery.

One cannot escape the effect of one's past karma. But then, if a person leads a prayerful life, he gets off with only the prick of a thorn in the leg, whereas he was to suffer from a deep cut.

One must perform work. It is only through work that the bondage of work will be cut asunder and one will acquire a spirit of non-attachment. One should not be without work even for a moment.

Prayer and meditation, or pilgrimage, or even earning money, all these should be done during the earlier part of one's life.

See what a tiny seed is the Name of God. From it in time come divine moods, devotion, love, and spiritual consummation.

When a man passes into a favourable time, he gets the desire to contemplate on God. But when the time is unfavourable, he gets all the facilities for doing evil actions. Everything happens in time according to the will of God.

There is no happiness while living in this body. The world is full of sorrow. Happiness is only an empty word. Only those who have received the grace of the Master can recognize him as God, and that is their real joy.

Do the Master's work, and along with that practise spiritual disciplines too. Work helps one to keep off idle thoughts. If one is without work, such thoughts rush into one's mind.

How can one's mind be healthy if one doesn't work? No one can spend all twenty-four hours in thought and meditation. So one must engage oneself in work; it keeps the mind cheerful.

You will gain everything if you but take refuge in the Master. Renunciation alone was his splendour. We utter his name and eat and enjoy things because he renounced all. He was a man of such complete renunciation.

The Master will be your protector. It will be a heinous sin on the part of the Master if he does not protect those who have taken shelter at his feet, who have taken refuge in him renouncing all, and who want to lead a good life.

If meditation is not possible, do japa. Realization will come through japa. If the meditative mood comes, well and good, but by no means do it by force.

You must give each one his due share of honour. Even a broom must be shown some honour. The smallest work must be done with reverence.

The result of Karma is inevitable. But by repeating the Name of God, you can lessen its intensity. If you were destined to have a wound as wide as a ploughshare, you will get a pin-prick at least. The effect of Karma can be counteracted to a great extent by japa and austerities.

An unmarried person who leads a pure life will advance towards Him with rapid strides, whether he prays to Him or not. The others, being tied hand and foot, find it difficult to extricate themselves from the bondage of worldliness, even though they try to think of God.

There can be no greater purifier of the mind and heart than meditation on the significance of the Mother's life. In the history of the world there is no parallel to the Holy Mother, because she was a unique incarnation of the Divine Shakti.

T.M.P. Mahadevan

Let me tell you how to love all equally. Do not demand anything of those you love. If you make demands, some will give you more and some less. In that case you will love more those who give you more and less those who give you less. Thus your love will not be the same for all. You will not be able to love all impartially.

Just as clouds are blown away by the wind, so the thirst for material pleasure will be driven away by the utterance of the Lord's name.

God is one's very 'own'. It is the eternal relationship. He is everyone's 'own'. One realizes Him in proportion to the intensity of one's feeling for Him.

Even a blade of grass cannot stir without the will of God. When a creature falls on good times, his thoughts turn to prayer; when he falls on bad times, all is evil. It is all according to God's will. It is God alone who expresses His will through the actions of man.

If you pray to him constantly before his picture, then he manifests himself through that picture. The place where the picture is kept becomes a shrine. Suppose a man worships the Master there (pointing to a plot of land), then the place is associated with his presence.

Though one gets a new body on account of desires, yet one does not completely lose spiritual consciousness if one has to one's credit merits from previous births.

When a man sees defects in others, his own mind first gets polluted. What does he gain by finding faults in others? He only hurts himself by that.

As you smell the fragrance of a flower while handling it or the smell of sandalwood while rubbing it against a stone, so you obtain spiritual awakening by constantly thinking of God. If you become desireless you can realize Him right now.

The mind will be steadied if one repeats the Name of God fifteen or twenty thousand times a day. It is truly so. I myself have experienced it. Let them practise it first; if they fail, let them complain.

You must work, of course. Work keeps the mind in order. But japa, meditation and prayer are quite essential. At least once at dawn and dusk one must sit down for spiritual practices.

Do you think I can be free so long as a single person of whom I have taken charge remains in bondage? I shall have to be with them all. I have taken the responsibility for their well-being.

It is idle to expect that dangers and difficulties will not come. They are bound to come. But for a devotee they will pass away under the feet like water.

While repeating the Name of God, if one sees His form and becomes absorbed in Him, one's japa stops. One gets everything when one succeeds in meditation.

Even water, which has a natural tendency to flow downwards, is drawn up to the sky by the sun's rays. In the same way, God's grace lifts up the mind which has got a tendency to run after sense objects.

Everything is illusory—husband, wife, even this body. These are the great shackles of maya. Unless you can free yourself from these shackles you will never be able to cross to the other shore of the world.

After the whole day's labour if you eat something and drink some water, the body will be quite refreshed. Thereafter, be it in japa, meditation or any other work, the mind will settle down quite steadily.

What will you gain by merely making so much of Swadeshi? Whatever we may be, we are rooted in the Master. He is our ideal. Whatever you do, if you keep a firm hold on the Master, nothing will go wrong.

The grace of God is the thing that is needful. One should pray for the grace of God. One must pray sitting on the bank of the river. One will be taken across in proper time.

As you progress in your spiritual practice you will see the same Being in you as in me, and that He is in all beings, be they of the lowest caste. Then you will acquire humility.

My child [replying to the question why she worked so hard], I have done much more than is necessary to make my life a model.

Those who have come here, those who are my children, have already achieved liberation. Even God can do no harm to my children!

When you sit at dusk, you get to think of all that you have done and not done during the day. Then you have to compare the states of your mind yesterday and today. Then doing japa one has to meditate on the form of one's Ishta.

First offer to God whatever you eat. One must not eat unoffered food. As your food is, so will be your blood. From pure food you get pure blood, pure mind and strength. Pure mind begets ecstatic love.

You bear children every year; you haven't even a little self-control. What is the good of coming to me and saying, 'What is the way out?'

Kali, the Mother of the universe, is the Mother of all. It is She alone who has begotten both good and evil. Everything has come out of Her womb.

If the mind is kept engaged in some work, it doesn't indulge in silly thoughts. But if you sit idle, the mind is likely to indulge in various kinds of thoughts.

Nothing can happen without the will of God. Not even a blade of grass can move. Everything happens in time according to the will of God.

When worldly thoughts crop up in your mind, and they possess it, then you should go away from the company of others and pray to Him with tears in your eyes. He will remove all the dross of your mind, and will also give you understanding.

When I used to stay in the Nahabat, on moonlit nights I would look at the reflection of the moon in the still waters of the Ganges and, weeping, pray to God, 'There are stains even on the moon, but let my mind be absolutely stainless.'

My child, if you can get perfect knowledge through my blessings then I bless you with all my heart and soul. Is it ever possible for a man to free himself unaided, from the clutches of Maya?

It was for this that the Master performed spiritual austerities to the utmost extent and gave the results thereof for the redemption of mankind.

'Holy Mother!' What an inspiring and uplifting epithet! Holy she was, being always in contact with that great and holy Sri Ramakrishna Paramahamsa, ever listening to the upadesha and serving him ever.

Sister R.S. Subbulakshmi

If you don't call upon God — indeed many people never even remember Him — what does it matter to Him? It is your own misfortune. Such is the maya of God, He keeps them ignorant of Him saying, 'They are happy enough, let them be so!'

An unmarried person is half-free, whether he prays to God or not. He will advance towards Him with rapid strides when he feels a little drawn towards Him.

Nonetheless, the mind naturally dwells on one's daily activities. If you don't succeed in meditation, practise japa. Japa leads to perfection. One attains perfection through japa.

There is no such rule that God's grace will fall on him simply because he is practising austerities. It entirely depends on His will.

There is no happiness whatever in human birth. The world is verily filled with misery. Happiness here is only a name.

Repetition of His name will lead to the goal. Even when your mind does not become concentrated you can repeat the Holy Name thousands of times.

During one's illness if one promises an offering to the guardian deity, one becomes free of danger. Besides, everybody should be given what is his due.

Think of me as one with him (Sri Ramakrishna). He is here inthisbodyinasubtleform.TheMasterhimselfdeclared, 'I shall live within you in a subtle form.'

Do you know that the Master looked upon all in this world as Mother? He left me behind this time for demonstrating that Motherhood to the world.

One realizes God in proportion to the intensity of one's feeling for Him. He who is really eager to cross the ocean of the world will somehow break his bonds. No one can entangle him.

There should be a regular time for the practice of japa and meditation. For no one knows when the auspicious moment will come. It comes suddenly—one has no hint of it beforehand.

The aim of life is to realize God and remain immersed in contemplation of Him. God alone is real and everything else is false.

Along with work, if you do not meditate morning and evening, how can you understand whether you are working on the right lines?

If my son wallows in the dust or mud, it is I who have to wipe all the dirt off his body and take him to my lap.

The rich should serve God and His devotees with money, and the poor should worship God by repeating His Name.

Husband, son, body, or whatever it be, is all in maya. All these are maya's bondage. One cannot be freed unless one gets rid of bondage.

Who has this faith that He is his 'own'? All practise these or those disciplines because they think it their duty to do so. But how many seek God?

The chief characteristic of the Master's sadhana was his renunciation. Has anyone ever seen such natural renunciation? Renunciation is his great ornament.

One must not speak unpleasant truths unnecessarily. By indulging in rude words one's nature becomes rude. One loses sensitivity without control over one's words.

Did the cowherd boys of Brindavan get Sri Krishna as their 'own' through japa or meditation? They realized Him through ecstatic love. They used to say to Him, as to an intimate friend, 'Come here, O Krishna! Eat this! Take this!'

The Master is really God who assumed a human body to remove the sufferings of men. He moved about just as a king walks through his city in disguise, and he left the world as soon as his identity was discovered.

Suppose one of my children has smeared himself with dirt. It is I, and no one else, who shall have to wash him clean and take him in my arms. To make mistakes is man's very nature; but few of those who criticize know how to correct them.

My child, several among those who come here are up to anything in life. No type of sin has been left untouched by them. But when they come here and address me as Mother, I forget everything and they get more than they deserve.

One needs good fortune, indeed, to accept the ideal of renunciation taught by the Master. How few can be rescued from the world once they are entangled in it!

The world is the Lord's. He created it for His own play. We are mere pawns in His game. Wherever He keeps us and in whatever way He does so, we have to abide by it contentedly.

Sri Ramakrishna was all Advaita and preached Advaita. Why should you not also follow Advaita? All his disciples are Advaitins.

[To sincere lay disciples] Is the ochre robe everything? You will realize God without it. What is the need of taking the ochre robe.

[Regarding Yogasanas] Be a little careful about it. If you continue such exercises for a long time, the mind may be diverted to the body. Again, if you give it up, it may affect your health. Therefore you should exercise your discretion.

Do you think that even if this body passes away, I can have any release unless every one of those whose responsibility I have taken on myself is out of bondage? I must constantly live with them. I have taken complete charge of everything, good or bad, regarding them.

It is my prayer, O Lord, that those who give up the world for your sake may not suffer for want of simple food and coarse clothing.

The Malaya breeze is blowing here. He who will unfurl his sail and take refuge in the Master will be blessed indeed.

Her mother's heart took in all castes, all lands, all faiths. The children of the East and the children of the West were her children without distinction or disparagement.

A Western Devotee

Keep a photo of the Master with you and know for certain that he is very near you. Pour out your heart's grief by shedding tears before him. Cry and pray earnestly. By repeatedly doing this you will find peace of mind.

Have faith in the Master and turn to him in prayer whenever you feel distraught.

One must have reverence for one's Guru... One's chance of salvation lies in one's reverence for him. Observe how the disciples of the Master revere him. Out of this reverence for him they revere not only all the members of his family, but even the cats from his home district!

We suffer as a result of our own actions; it is unfair to blame anybody for it. We have to surrender ourselves completely to the Lord with faith and devotion in Him, serve others to the best of our capacity and never be a source of sorrow to anybody.

The mind keeps well when engaged in work. And yet japa, meditation, prayers also are specially needed. You must at least sit down once in the morning and again in the evening. That acts as a rudder to a boat.

Suppose someone tells you about his good and evil deeds. Every time you think of that person you must perforce remember his good and evil deeds. In this manner his good and evil deeds both leave some impression upon your mind.

You may talk of the vision of God, or of meditation, but remember, the mind is everything. One gets everything when the mind becomes steady.

Is it a trifle to give initiation? What a tremendous responsibility have we to accept! How much anxiety have we to suffer for them!

Don't be afraid. Human birth is full of suffering and one has to endure everything patiently, taking the Name of God. None, not even God in human form, can escape the sufferings of the body and mind.

Even Avataras, saints and sages have to undergo the ordeal of suffering, for they take upon themselves the burden of sins of omission and commission of ordinary human beings and thereby sacrifice themselves for the good of humanity.

Mark you, my dear, modesty is the greatest ornament of a woman. A flower best serves its purpose when it is offered to a deity; else it may as well wither on the plant.

While repeating the name of God, if one sees His form and becomes absorbed in Him, one's japa stops. One gets everything when one succeeds in meditation.

So long as the ego exists, desires also undoubtedly remain. But those desires will not injure you. The Master will be your protector.

You are my own people. But remember this, that an educated Sadhu, is like an elephant whose tusks are covered with gold.

The mind is by nature restless. Therefore, at the outset, to make the mind steady, one may practise meditation by regulating the breathing a little. That helps to steady the mind. But one must not overdo it. That heats the brain.

When one sits in meditation in the evening, one gets a chance to think of what one has done—good or bad—during the whole day. Next one should compare the state of one's mind in the preceding day and the present.

Before the awakening of the Kundalini, one hears the Anahata sound; but nothing can be achieved without the grace of the Divine Mother.

My child, this world is like a deep marshy place. Once a man gets entangled there, it becomes very difficult for him to come out.

How can they [get rid of desires]? If they could, then the creation would come to an end. The world is going on because not all can be free of desires. People with desires are born again and again.

Any movement in the air disturbs the steady burning of the flame; even so the presence of any thought or desire makes the mind unsteady. The Mantra must be correctly repeated. An incorrect utterance delays progress.

It is the nature of water to flow downwards, but the sun's rays lift it up towards the sky; likewise it is the very nature of the mind to go to lower things, to objects of enjoyment, but the grace of God can make the mind go towards higher objects.

Repeat the name of God. If you do so, He will cut away your bondage some day. Can anyone get liberation, my child, unless He Himself removes the shackles? Have deep faith in God. Look upon the Master as your refuge, even as children regard their parents.

The Kundalini will be gradually awakened. You will realize everything by the repetition of God's Name. Even if the mind is not quite, still you can sit and repeat the holy name a million times.

Do not waste time in calculating and worrying whether or not you are progressing in the path of spirituality. It is egoistic to judge progress for oneself. Have faith in the grace of your Guru and Ishta.

If the moon in the sky be covered with clouds, the wind blows them away; and then only you can see the moon. Do the clouds scatter away all of a sudden? Exactly the same here. The Karmas get exhausted slowly. When God is realized, He illumines the soul internally-one knows this internally.

Everyone should serve his mother. It is all the more incumbent upon you [monks], because you have all come to me with purpose of dedicating your life to the service of others... Always talk to her about God. You will really fulfil the duty of a son if you can help her to gather the means for her ultimate journey.

What is after all in this body? Why should one become enmeshed in this Maya? It will ultimately come to an end after a few days. Then when it is burnt, there will remain only a seer and a half of ash.

It is my prayer that my children should live together, clinging to [the Master] and [his] teachings, and people afflicted with the sufferings of the world should come to them and get peace of mind by hearing from them [his] words.

I have seen in Vrindavan and Banaras so many holy men living on alms and having the shade of trees for shelter. There is no lack of sadhus of that type. I cannot bear to see my children, who have renounced all for [Master's] sake, wandering about for a morsel of food.

(Regarding earning money and accumulating it by the householders) You have your wife and children. You should lay by something for them... Besides, you will be able to serve the holy men too. If you have nothing, what will you give to the holy men, my dear?

The Master used to say that the worldly person is like a spring mattress—sit on it and it goes down, but the moment you get up, it springs back at once. The regard and devotion for God of these worldly men is just like a drop of water on a hot plate—it evaporates in no time.

Tender welcome awaited all who sought her whether from East or West. All alike were her children. Hers was an all-embracing mother-heart which wrapped itself in love about every child born of woman, and her family was the human race...

Sister Devamata

The mind is rendered pure as the result of many austerities. 'God who is purity itself cannot be attained without austerities.' What else does one obtain by the realization of God? Does he grow two horns? No, his mind becomes pure, and through a pure mind one attains knowledge and spiritual awakening.

Once a man casts all consideration for others to the winds, he stops at nothing. The Master would say, 'If you have to ask a lame man how he became lame, then you have to speak thus: "How did your leg come to such a condition?"'

*Prophets and Incarnations are born to show benighted humanity their way. They give different instructions to suit different temperaments. There are many ways to realize truth.
So all these instructions have their relative value.*

To question too much is not good. It is difficult to properly assimilate even one thought. Now why should you trouble your mind by harbouring ten thoughts? Dive deep with the noble idea that you have received. Repeat the Holy Name, meditate upon it, keep good company, and subdue the ego by all means.

Always discriminate. Whenever the mind goes after anything other than God, consider it as transient and surrender the mind at the sacred feet of the Lord. Be like the man who, while angling for fish, became so absorbed in it that he did not hear the least of the din and bustle of a marriage procession passing by.

Repeat the name of God in the innermost core of your heart and in all sincerity take refuge in the Master. Do not bother to know how your mind is reacting to things around.

It is wrong if the mind is drawn towards secular objects. By 'secular objects' is meant money, family, etc. But it is natural to think of the work in which one is engaged.

From time out of mind innumerable people have worshiped images and thus attained spiritual knowledge. Can you deny this fact? The Master never cherished dogmatic views.

Now that you are with [me], what's the need of so much japa and meditation? I, indeed, am doing everything for you. Now eat and live merrily, free from all care.

Certainly you will have doubts. There will be questionings and faith will return again. That is how faith is established.

One should always recollect God and pray to Him for right understanding. How many are there who can meditate and practice japa all that time? At first they earnestly practice these disciplines, but their brains become heated in the long run by sitting constantly.

By praying to Him constantly one gets ecstatic love (Prema Bhakti) through His grace. This Prema, my child, is the innermost thing of spiritual life.

Alas, how much did I weep and pray to the Master for my children! That is why you find everywhere ashramas and monasteries through his blessings.

How have they known as to what will give success and what will not? Does one achieve everything by practicing japa and meditation for a few days? Nothing whatever is achieved unless Mahamaya clears the path.

Didn't you notice the other day that a person's brain became deranged because he forced himself to excessive prayer and meditation? If one's head becomes deranged, one's life becomes useless. The intelligence of a man is very precarious.

It is much better to work than to allow the mind to roam at large. For when the mind gets a free scope to wander, it creates much confusion. My Naren thought of these things and wisely founded institutions where people would do disinterested work.

Even if the mind is not concentrated, do not give up the repetition of the Holy Word. You do your duty. While repeating the Name, the mind will get fixed of itself on the ideal, like a candle flame in a place protected from the wind.

If you repeat with an eye to number, your mind may be concentrated on the number alone. Therefore I would advise you to repeat the Name of God without being particular about the number.

Whether you jump into water or are pushed into it, your cloth will get drenched. Is it not so? Meditate every day... Constant meditation will make the mind one-pointed. Discriminate always between the real and the unreal.

When God first created man, He endowed him with the spirit of goodness. As a result, men were born with wisdom and it did not take them long to realize that the world was an ephemeral thing. Immediately they took the Name of God and set out to meditate on Him and by His grace were liberated from the bonds of life.

You may think that you have no attachment for money, that since you have renounced it once for all you will not get attached to it, that you will be able to be free from it whenever you wish. Oh, no! Never harbour such an idea in your mind. Money will find its way somehow to grip you unawares by the neck, as it were.

Discriminate always between the real and the unreal. Whenever you find your mind drawn to any object, think of its transitoriness, and thus try to withdraw the mind back to the thought of God.

A man was angling. A bridal party was going along the road with music. But the angler's eye remained fixed on the float. The mind of a spiritual aspirant should be steadfast like that.

It is Nature's law [the weaknesses of the mind], just as you find the full moon and the new moon. Similarly the mind is possessed of noble thoughts at times and haunted by evil thoughts at other moments.

Men can hardly earn money through honest means, and even this contaminates their mind very much... Money is such a thing that one develops an attachment for it, if one is associated with it for long!

If you want peace of mind, do not find fault with others. Rather see your own faults. Learn to make the whole world your own. No one is a stranger. The whole world is your own.

My child, I bless you from my heart that you live long, attain devotion, and enjoy peace. Peace is the principal thing. One needs peace alone.